Christmas

Ultimate Sticker and Activity Collection

Jane Bull

DK

LONDON, NEW YORK, MUNICH,
MELBOURNE, and DELHI

Design Jane Bull
Design assistance Poppy Joslin,
Sonia Moore, Wendy Bartlet
Editor Lee Wilson
US editor Margaret Parrish
Jacket design Sonia Moore
Photography Andy Crawford
Category publisher Mary Ling
Production editor Andy Hilliard
Production controller Emma Sparks

Content first published in *The Christmas
Book* (2001), *The Cooking Book* (2002), *The
Rainy Day Book* (2003) *The Crafty Art Book*
(2004), *The Merry Christmas Activity Book*
(2005), and *The Baking Book* (2005).

This edition published in the United States
in 2012 by DK Publishing
375 Hudson Street
New York, New York 10014

12 13 14 15 16 10 9 8 7 6 5 4 3 2 1
001–186491–September/12
A catalog record for this book is
available from the Library of Congress.
ISBN: 978-0-7566-9902-4

Color reproduction by MDP, UK
Printed and bound by L Rex, China

Discover more at **www.dk.com**

Contents

Let's decorate

Make an advent box-calendar and count down to Christmas. Create ornaments and pom-poms, mobiles and string things, hanging stars and paper snowflakes to decorate your home and Christmas tree.

Christmas Countdown

The buildup to Christmas will never be the same again with this 3-D, advent box-calendar. It'll help the days fly by!

Discover the delights in every drawer

8

No more boxes left to open? It must be Christmas!

HOW TO MAKE YOUR ADVENT BOX

All you need for this spectacular advent box-calendar is one large cereal box and 23 little boxes. On the first of December open the main doors, then each day until Christmas Eve open a box to reveal a surprise.

Ask an adult. . .
for help with the spraying

Cut down the center of a cereal box to create doors.

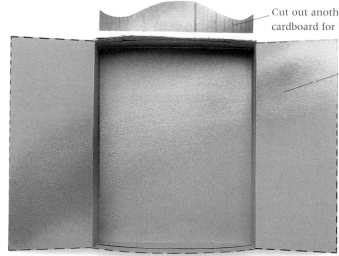

Cut out another piece of cardboard for the decorative top.

Color the inside and outside with gold spray paint.

Cut out a star and glue it on the top of the box.

Stick flat boxes on the inside of the doors. Check that the doors can shut fully.

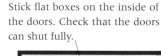

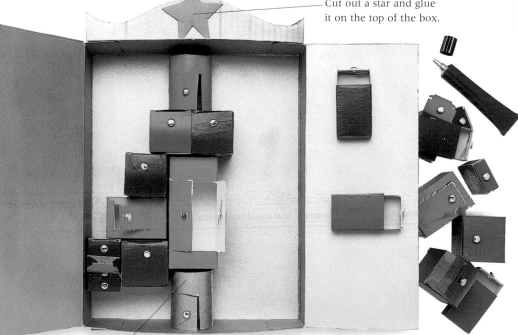

Glue the boxes in place—you can create any Christmas shape you like with them.

Decorate the calendar with torn pieces of foil and glue a star on each little box to write the numbers on.

CANDY WRAPPERS   TORN FOIL   STICKERS   TREE SHAPES   CRAFT GLUE

10

Collect 23 little boxes to put inside

Try out different arrangements with the boxes.

Paint the boxes with acrylic paint and craft glue mixed together.

Cut doors in the boxes and use paper fasteners as handles.

Drape tinsel around the box for an extra sparkle, and decorate the star.

Tie on a cardboard star with the number "1" on it.

Open one box a day until Christmas!

Fill the boxes with goodies—candy, jokes, messages, or toys.

Glue down small, plastic bottle caps for handles.

Tie a bow onto the doors to keep them shut.

Write the numbers on each box, from 2 to 24.

Snowy bunting

Deck your walls
with flurries of snowflakes and
streamers of happy snowmen.

13

How to make snowy bunting

The trick with this bunting is to take a piece of string, then thread your decorations onto it with a straw between each one to separate them. Try these simple ideas.

OLD GREETING CARDS

...Take some old cards and cut them into shapes.

Paper snow

Turn to page 24 for instructions on how to make snowflakes, then string them up for a flurry of festive fun.

STRAWS

Punch a hole in the paper snow.

STRING

SINGLE HOLE PUNCHER

LOTS OF PAPER SNOW SHAPES

Paper plate flakes

Now make colorful snowflakes and attach them to paper plates, or turn the plates into smiling snowmen.

HOLE PUNCHER

STRAWS

SCISSORS

GLUE STICK

PAPER

STRING

PAPER PLATES

Cut the snowman's face out of paper or posterboard and glue it on.

PAPER SNOW

Glue the paper snow onto the plates.

14

Snowy greetings

Don't throw them out! Last year's greeting cards make instant colorful decorations. Cut the cards into shapes, punch a hole in them, and string them up with straws in between to separate them.

Thread the snowflakes on the string with straws between them.

STRAWS

STRING

Punch holes in the plates.

Thread string through the straws and the holes in the plates.

Remember to knot the ends so everything stays on.

Ornaments,

stars, and 3-D trees

Make them small to hang on a tree

or huge to hang from the ceiling.

Whatever you do, hang them up!

16

3-D trees

For a 3-D look, slot two shapes together. Try two circles as well to give an ornamental effect.

1. Cut two tree shapes exactly the same size.

Cut a slot in one tree from the top to halfway down.

2. Now cut a slot in the other tree.

Cut from base to halfway up.

3. Slide one shape onto the other.

4. Stand your tree up, or glue on some thread and hang it on the tree.

If you use old, recycled Christmas cards, all the decorations will be completely different. You can also use your homemade printed paper.

Little or large

Add a string and hang me up

How to make ornaments and stars

For ornaments you will need

Old greeting cards • Thick paper • Ruler • Pen • Scissors • Hole puncher • Paper fasteners • Thread

REUSE OLD GREETING CARDS

Ornaments

PENCIL

SCISSORS

SINGLE HOLE PUNCHER

Punch the holes at the bottom and the top.

1 Cut the card into strips.

2 Punch holes.

Tie thread around the paper fastener to hang it up.

Clip the strips together at the bottom and the top.

PAPER FASTENERS

3 Clip together.

4 Fan out the strips to form a ball.

Use a piece of paper measuring
8½ in (22 cm) x 11 in (28 cm).

1 Take a piece of paper.

Fold the paper backward and
forward like an accordion.
Make the folds about 1 in
(2 cm) wide.

Fold the
folded paper
in half.

2 Fold it into pleats.

Unfold the paper and
draw lines to show
where to cut the holes.

3 Cut holes.

Fan out the paper
and tape the sides
together.

4 Tape the edge.

Tape the other side to
complete the circle,
then add a piece of
string to hang it up.

5 It's a star!

Winter woollies

Soft and squashy felt decorations hang around with fuzzy pom-poms.

How to stitch some woollies

Collect colorful felt fabric and thread. Cut out two shapes, sew them together using blanket stitch, stuff them with soft wadding, and decorate with sparkly sequins. Turn to page 42 to make pompoms.

NEEDLE-THREADER

GOLD OR SILVER THREAD

LOTS OF DIFFERENT COLORED FELT

SEQUINS AND RIBBONS FOR DECORATION

Needles and pins

You will need:
• embroidery needles (use a needle-threader to help you thread a needle)
• Glue
• Stuffing

PINS

COLORED EMBROIDERY FLOSS OR THIN YARN

WHITE GLUE

POLYFILL

SCISSORS

Cutting shapes

For templates, draw shapes on a piece of cardboard.

Cover the page with a piece of tracing paper.

Trace over the shapes with a pencil.

Glue a heart to the triangle shape.

Angels and fairies

Cut out, stitch, and stuff

Pin your template onto a piece of folded felt and cut it out.

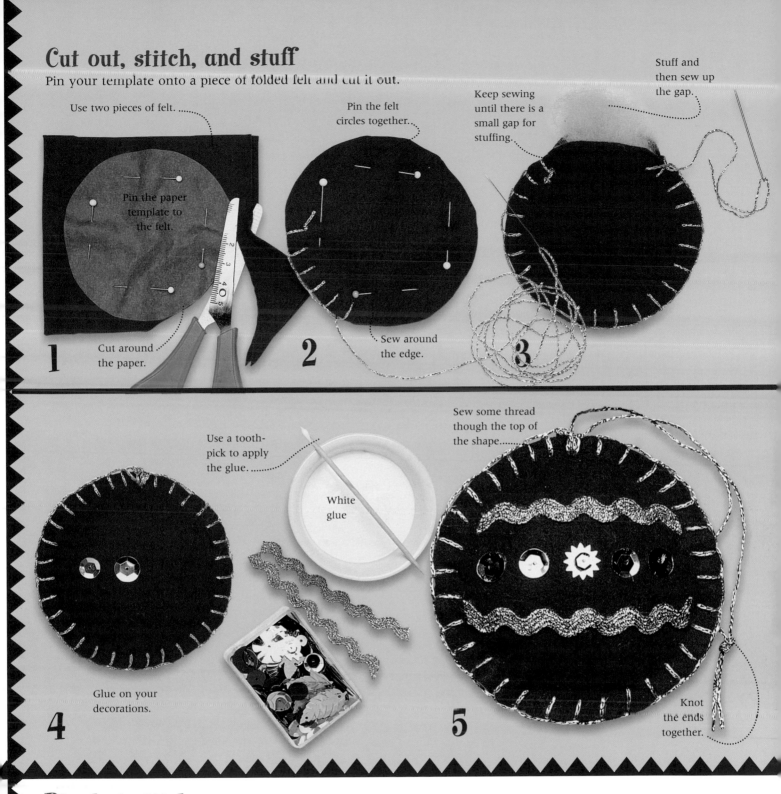

Use two pieces of felt.

Pin the paper template to the felt.

1 Cut around the paper.

Pin the felt circles together.

2 Sew around the edge.

Keep sewing until there is a small gap for stuffing.

Stuff and then sew up the gap.

3

Use a tooth-pick to apply the glue.

White glue

Sew some thread though the top of the shape.

4 Glue on your decorations.

Knot the ends together.

5

Blanket stitch   This stitch looks great and is easy to do, but keep it neat!

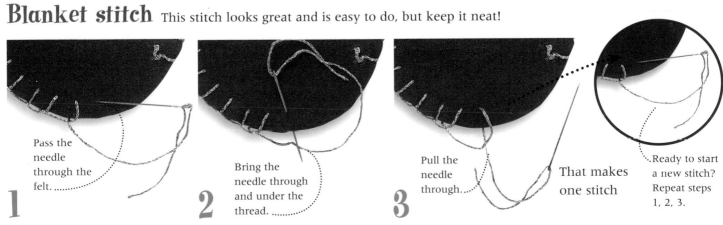

1 Pass the needle through the felt.

2 Bring the needle through and under the thread.

3 Pull the needle through...

That makes one stitch

Ready to start a new stitch? Repeat steps 1, 2, 3.

Paper Snow

A flurry of paper snowflakes

float and swirl through the sky, settling in the branches of the trees.

Take a piece of paper and fold it in half twice along the dotted lines.

Your paper will look like this.

Fold it in half again.

Now snip away, then unfold the flake.

Hang up your snowflake with thread.

Snowstorms of snowflakes!

See what shapes unfold

Get wrapped up in these paper pom-poms

Ornaments, Orbs, and Pom-poms

Ornaments for the tree; orbs to hang from the ceiling.

26

Hang out with me and my spinning decorations

Transform flat cards into shapely spheres

✦ Hanging Around

Glittering ornaments and giant orbs
swinging and spinning around your room give
it a magical Christmassy feel. All you need are old comic
strips, wrapping paper, greeting cards, postcards, or
anything else that's bright—just get permission to cut it up!

27

Paper Pom-poms

Pom-poms can be made out of any paper you like. Christmas wrapping paper is cheery and bright, or you can decorate your own paper with a Christmas pattern using paint or stickers.

Cut out eight disks of paper (about template size below).

Fold the bunch of disks in half and staple down the crease.

Ornaments

Festive ornaments can be hung on trees or simply left to spin from ceilings. When you have mastered the ornament, try making a spectacular, giant orb with 20 decorated paper plates. Good luck finding room for something that big!

Take a stack of old Christmas cards and trace around the template.

Cut out 20 circles, and snip out the notches (see template).

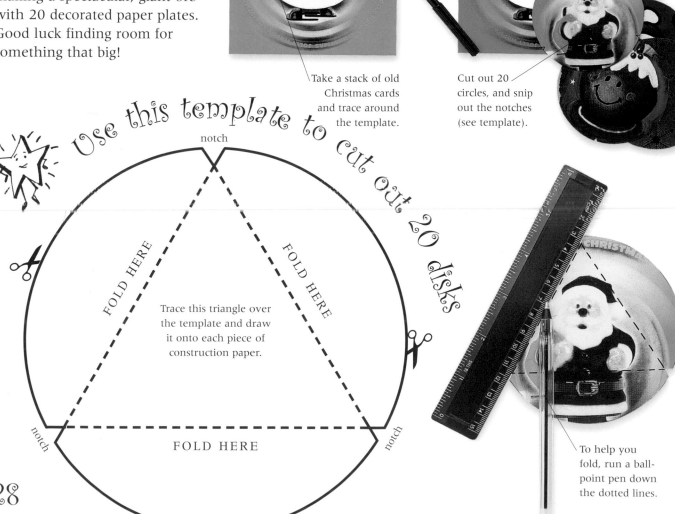

Use this template to cut out 20 disks

notch

FOLD HERE

FOLD HERE

Trace this triangle over the template and draw it onto each piece of construction paper.

notch

FOLD HERE

notch

To help you fold, run a ballpoint pen down the dotted lines.

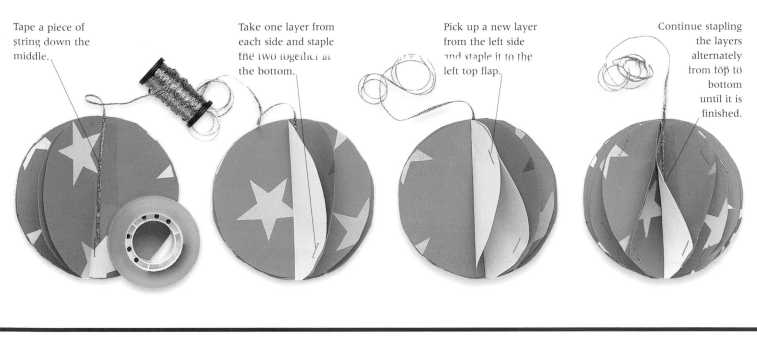

Tape a piece of string down the middle.

Take one layer from each side and staple the two together at the bottom.

Pick up a new layer from the left side and staple it to the left top flap.

Continue stapling the layers alternately from top to bottom until it is finished.

Staple the flaps together at each end. Keep stapling them together until they become an orb shape.

To hang up your ornament, make a hole and tie some string through it.

Make a giant orb using 20 paper plates.

Wow! it's almost as big as me!

Decorate your tree with glittering goodies

Tree Art

There's nothing better than a tree covered in colorful decorations to remind you that it's Christmas. It's even better if you have made them all yourself!

Turn me into a dangling tree ornament

Ping-pong-ball angel heads, dangling Santas, glittering ornaments, yogurt cup goody baskets, a foil star—they look amazing and are simple to make, too.

Christmas Tree

Turn your bedroom into a festive delight by trimming a tree with an explosion of colorful ornaments.

HOW TO MAKE TREE ORNAMENTS

Salt Dough Dangles

2¹/₂ cups all-purpose flour
1 cup salt
1 cup water
1 teaspoon oil

Put all of the ingredients into a bowl and dig in.

Squeeze it together to make a ball of dough.

Cut out shapes with a cookie cutter or a knife.

Cook for 20 minutes at 350°F (180°C).
Cool on a wire rack before painting.

Don't forget to make a hole in each with a toothpick before you cook them, so that you can hang them up.

Make a base and pinch off pieces of dough to make features.

Ask an adult. . .
to help with the oven

Delicious as they look, these decorations aren't very tasty!

Ho, ho, ho!

32

Make Santa's dough head

Remember the hole.

Build his face

Heat him up

Add some string.

Color him in

Glitter Card Dangles

All you need for these sparkling dangles is some cardboard and lots of decorations—go wild with the sequins!

Draw some shapes on a piece of cardboard.

Cut out the shapes.

Make a hole in the top with a toothpick.

Glue on some colored foil and sequins.

Thread some string through the hole.

Add more and more sequins!

Candy Cups

Fill this doll-sized basket, made out of a yogurt cup, with tasty treats.

Cut off the rim.

Glue on a ribbon handle.

Decorate and fill with candies. Yummy!

Angel Head

Transform a cheap ping-pong ball into a beautiful angel's face in seconds.

Make a hole at the top and bottom.

Thread string through and knot at the bottom.

Wind string around your fingers.

Tie it in the middle.

Cut the edges.

Glue the hair to the head.

Decorate the face.

Treetop

A cardboard star smothered in glittery candy wrappers finishes off your tree perfectly. Dress up your tree and make sure no one steals the candy!

Shredded foil candy wrappers.

Glue pieces of foil onto the cardboard star.

To hang it on the tree, attach a band of construction paper to the back with glue.

Decorate your tree with lots of glitzy colors!

Merry Mobiles

Christmas is on the move.

Hang Rudolphs, Santas, wintry snowmen, and tree faces around your room and you'll be spinning!

Cut out shapes from cardboard and jazz them up

Use cardboard for your mobiles.

Glitter will catch the light when the mobiles spin and give the room an extra sparkle.

Paint the eyes

These ornaments make great tree eyes.

Ping-pong ball eyes.

Give the nose an extra sparkle

Make a hole at the top and bottom, thread some string through, and knot.

Watch Rudolph try to catch his nose!

Feeling dizzy yet?

It's meltdown for the snowman!

In a Spin

Hang these fantastic mobiles from the ceiling and watch them spinning and twirling around. Remember to paint and decorate them on both sides so that whichever way they turn you can see exactly what they are.

35

Storm in a Jelly Jar

Shake up the snow!

Catch some Christmas magic and keep it in a jar.

Wow! These sparkle more than me!

HOW TO MAKE A SWIRLING SNOWSTORM

For your stormy winter wonderlands, all you need are some screw-top jars, water, glycerine, glitter, and a few toys. Add them together, and you have a perfect gift for all the movers and shakers you know!

shake, whirl, and swirl!

★ Take a Jar

Choose a small jar with a very tight, screw-top lid. You may want to test it—you don't want your snowstorms to leak!

1

2

3

Add glitter first

GLYCERINE

PLASTIC TOY

WATER

STRONG GLUE

GLITTER

☆ Glycerine

Glycerine is a nontoxic liquid that can be bought in most pharmacies and craft stores. It slightly thickens the water so that your glitter-snow falls more slowly when you shake it. Use about one part glycerine to two parts water.

☆ Glue Tip

To attach the toy, use a strong glue that seals even when in water. For an extra seal, add glue around the lid and inside the rim. This prevents leakage.

No great shakes, they're easy to make

Glue around the inside of the lid and the outside of the jar rim.

Decorate the lid with festive ribbon.

4

5

string things

All wound up! From see-through string balls to fluffy pom-poms, there's a whole new woolly world to discover.

Juggle those
pom-poms!

How to make a string thing

You will need • Balloon • String or yarn • Wallpaper paste • Petroleum jelly

Blow up a balloon and spread petroleum jelly over it to keep the string from sticking to the balloon.

Mix up a bowl of wallpaper paste.

Cut a 22-in (60-cm) piece of string.

Dip the string into the paste, then wrap it around the balloon.

Add more and more and more string until you have enough.

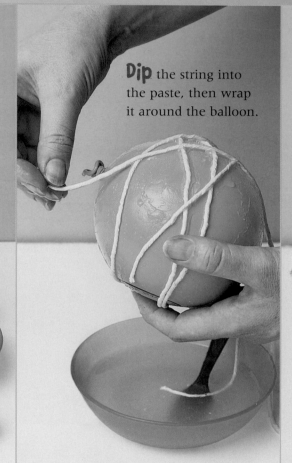

Inflated balloon

Wallpaper paste

Petroleum jelly

String

Watch out!
This part gets messy

Leave it to dry overnight

How to make a pom-pom

You will need • Thin cardboard • Yarn

Tip: The larger the disks, the bigger your pom-pom will be.

Knot the yarn in place.

Add more yarn until it's completely covered

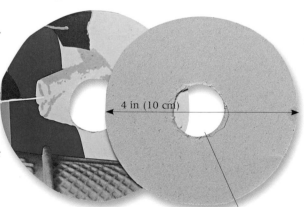

4 in (10 cm)

Cut out two cardboard disks.

Cut a 1-in (2.5-cm) hole in the middle of each disk.

Put the two disks together.

Wind the yarn around and around, through the middle and over the top.

When the string is dry...

pop the balloon!

Put the scissors between the two disks.

Snip the yarn all the way around.

Hold it firmly in the middle.

Open up the disks slightly.

Tie a piece of yarn tightly around the middle.

Tip For multicolor pom-poms, add diffferent yarn as you wind.

Trim off any long pieces.

Pull the disk off and fluff up the yarn.

A pom-pom—it's magic!

43

Christmas night

Hush now, all is quiet.

Light your lanterns and watch them twinkle in the dark to welcome festive friends.

Four decorative designs

When the candle burns, it can reveal a host of angels, colorful spots, stained-glass shapes, or a starlit skyscape. All you need is a jelly jar and tissue paper.

Alternatively, glue tissue-paper circles onto your tracing paper.

3 Tissue paper

Cut out some blue tissue paper the same size as the tracing paper, draw stars, and cut them out.

2 Cut out a landscape from colored paper and glue it to the tracing paper.

4 Glue the blue paper to the back of the tracing paper.

Festive forest

1 Cut some tracing paper to fit around a jar.

5 Wrap the sheet around the jar.

Tape in position.

Shining star jar

1 Cut a piece of paper the height of the jar and long enough to fit around it.

2 Snip a zigzag along the top and draw and cut a pattern out of the middle.

3 Glue a different-colored piece of tissue paper to the back of the design and wrap the paper around the jar.

Glowing angels

Draw a design on the folded paper, and cut it out.

1 Fold a piece of paper in half, then half again, and then again.

2 Unfold the paper.

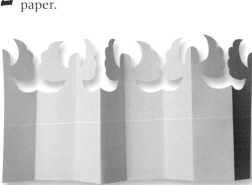

3 Make the paper into a crown shape and tape the ends together. Slip it over a large jar.

This design slips over a jar—it's not attached like the others.

Festive windows

Day and night, give your room a Christmassy glow with these tissue windows.

1

SCISSORS

PENCIL

Draw your picture on a sheet of dark-colored posterboard, and cut out some shapes.

2

Glue pieces of tissue to the back of the picture.

GLUE STICK

COLORED TISSUE PAPER

3 Turn your picture back over.

Now stick your silhouette in the window and let it shine out!

Clever cutouts

Instead of a picture, try cutting out a snowflake from folded paper.

Turn to page 24 to find out how to make one.

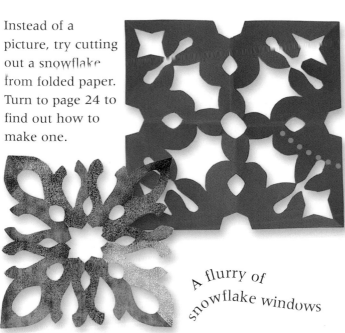

A flurry of snowflake windows

Frosty Welcomes

Light up the night before Christmas with shining ice decorations or glistening ice-bowl lanterns.

They're illuminating!

Make your garden glow
with Christmassy candlelight

A welcome glow for festive friends

HOW DOES YOUR YARD GLOW?

All you need for a Christmas glow is some seasonal cuttings, candles, and lots of ice. You can use anything wintry for your foliage, from holly and ivy to berries and cranberries—just get outside, start picking, and create a welcoming light outside in your yard.

⭐ The Big Freeze

Position a small bowl inside a larger one and tape it so that it is hanging in the center—not touching the bottom or sides. Fill the larger bowl with foliage and water, and freeze it.

If the small bowl bobs up too much put some pebbles in it to weigh it down.

⭐ Defrost Tip

To remove the bowls, you may have to dip the frozen lantern in warm water, and pour a little into the smaller bowl as well, to loosen the i

⭐ Ice Light

Use half a plastic bottle and a cup for the long lanterns, making sure that the cup doesn't touch the edges of the bottle at all. Use small or tall candles for the inside and if it starts to defrost, perk it up by putting it back into the freezer for a while.

Ask an adult . . .

⭐ to light the candles

1

2

Let it all hang out in the yard

Tape the string to the sides of the lid to stop it from moving while it freezes.

Ice Art

Find a lid or a tray with at least a 1/2-in- (1-cm-) tall rim and fill it with water. Put your plant decorations into it then drape the ends of a long piece of string in each side—they will freeze with the ice and can be used to hang it up.

4

5

Find a box your size

and ask an adult. . .

★ to cut three holes in it for your arms and head

Pass the Present

Do you have a Christmas hat? If so, put it on!

Decorate a headband with tinsel for an extra sparkle.

If you can fit your whole body into the box, it makes a very clever disguise.

Complete your outfit by carrying another package—you could fill it with candy.

54

All you need is a cardboard box to create a present party-piece to parade around in!

⭐ Wrap it Up

When you have your arm and head holes, simply wrap up the box using a roll of wrapping paper and adhesive tape.

⭐ Ribbons and Bows

To make ribbons and bows, cut long strips of paper and tape them around the box. Fold some extra strips into bow shapes and tape into position.

If you find a big enough box, keep your head inside and make a peephole at the front.

Why not wear a red Christmas outfit underneath your box?

55

That's Entertainment!

Family and friends like nothing more than to sit back, relax, and be entertained. So spoil them with a spectacular show.

You're a Star

Abracadabra!

Hey Presto!

Know any magic tricks? If so, then create a magician's costume and astonish your audience. If not, then tell a few jokes or a funny story.

I'll sing you a song

A little Song and Dance

Sing a few old favorites and encourage the audience to join in, or try your hand at one of the latest popular songs. When you have perfected the music, make up a dance routine for it.

Carol Singers

There's nothing better at Christmas than singing the Christmas carols everyone knows. Perform them at home or persuade an adult to take you out on a tour of the neighborhood. You can collect money for your favorite charity.

Hark the Herald Angels Sing

What a Performance!

⭐ Curtains Up!

Perform a play for your family and friends using various props and costumes. Try a puppet show using some old socks.

A round of applause for . . .

⭐ That's Show Business!

Making costumes is easier than you think! All you have to do is search around your house for odds and ends and use your imagination. You can create a costume horse with a rug and a cardboard box, or a fairy with a ballet outfit and a few homemade props. Invent your own story or simply tell an old favorite.

Hocus pocus, turn into a horse!

Welcome to the Christmas Quiz

Try hosting a game show for your family. Invent your own game rules and give away prizes—tempt the contestants with them at the beginning of the show. Make up your own questions or simply ask teams to race each other in simple tasks.

Take your seats please

The Christmas Show

Performed by:
The Festive players

Act One: Aunt Jill arrives
Act Two: Disaster Dessert
Intermission
Act Three: Jamie saves the day!
Grand Finale

Draw your own program for a show. Why not pretend to be members of your family and act out a family scene. Be careful not to upset anyone!

Cards and Gifts

Make some glitter cards and send 3-D greetings to your friends. Print some special wrapping paper and create containers and boxes for your Christmas gifts.

Glittery greetings

Pour on the glitter
and send a Christmas card
with added sparkle to your
special friends.

Get out your glitter

Gather up all the sparkly
things you can find:
Glitter • Glitter glue pens
Sequins • Jiggly eyes • Stickers
Gift ribbons • Tinsel
You'll also need posterboard,
a paintbrush, and some white glue.

Create a glitter card

Paintbrush

White glue

Fold a piece of posterboard in half.

Paint your design with glue.

Sprinkle on the glitter.

...down a sheet [of] newspaper [to] catch the [gli]tter.

Shake it off.

[Fin]ish your card [wi]th extra [de]corations, [su]ch as stickers [and] paint.

Don't waste any!

Fold the newspaper in half.

Pour the glitter back.

Cookie-cutter shapes

Any shape cutter will work.

white glue

Dip a cutter in glue, press it on the paper, then cover it with glitter.

piles of presents

Christmas Greetings

Greetings

From the 3rd Dimension

Big-nosed Rudolphs, 3-D snowmen, leaping stars, and a Santa bearing a bouncing gift.

They're out of this World!

Merry Christmas

Happy holidays

HOW TO MAKE 3-D GREETING CARDS

Make sure your card is the first to be noticed on the mantlepiece with these pop-up, springing, bobbing, greeting cards!

Open it up and out it pops

⭐ Template

These templates are for the Christmas tree, the snowman, and the presents. Cut the solid lines and fold the dotted lines. Trace them onto your folded construction paper.

Be careful not to draw your picture over half-way across the card or the fold will stick out too much when the card is closed.

⭐ 3-D, Festive, Fold-out Card

From a flat card to a pile of presents in a Christmas flash! Four simple cuts and your greeting cards are transformed. Try the snowman and Christmas tree designs, too.

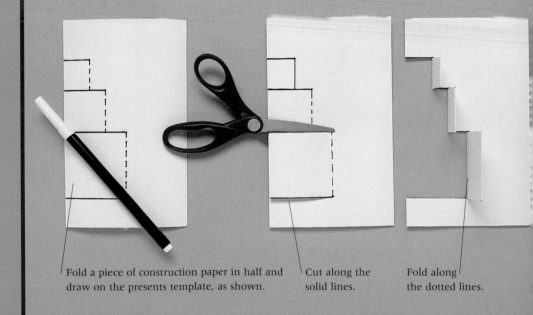

Fold a piece of construction paper in half and draw on the presents template, as shown.

Cut along the solid lines.

Fold along the dotted lines.

Pop-up Wobble Card

With this magic spring card, you can make anything appear to jump out at the person who receives it— from Rudolph's nose to Santa's present or a twinkling star. Try out some of your own designs. How about some springing, jangling bells, or a snowman spring?

Rudolph's nose

Cut out a piece of construction paper and fold it in half.

Cut Rudolph's face and nose out of two other colors of paper. Glue the face onto the main card.

Help Rudolph's nose wibble and wobble!

Draw a swirl on a piece of construction paper—no bigger than Rudolph's nose. Cut it out.

Glue the center of the spring to the back of the nose.

Glue the other end of the spring to Rudolph's face.

Complete Rudolph by drawing on his features.

Cut a piece of construction paper, slightly bigger than the original cutout piece.

Glue the construction paper to the backing piece, matching the folds in the middle.

Decorate the card with stickers or colored foil.

Special gifts

Wrap and tag

Dip it, print it, wrap it, tag it!
It's great to give gifts but
even better to give them
wrapped in homemade
paper, complete with
matching tags.

69

How to print

Clear a space. You are now going to do some big printing! Find some plain paper that is big enough for wrapping presents—a roll of brown craft paper is good—and start printing. Remember to make an extra stencil that you can cut out and turn into a matching tag.

Frosty, the potato man

Cut a potato in half, dab it in the paint, and press the potato onto the paper. Repeat for the body shape.

You will need:

• Sheets of plain paper

• Sponges

• Odds and ends for printing

• Acrylic paint

• Cardboard for the stencils

• Pen and scissors

• Ribbon or string to attach the tag

Shooting star stencils

Draw a star on a piece of paper.

Cut out the star.

Place the stencil on your wrapping paper. Dip the sponge into some paint and dab it over the stencil.

Take the stencil off carefully—you don't want the paint to smudge.

Spongy festive forest

Draw your shape on a sponge.

Cut it out.

Glue the sponge onto a piece of cardboard.

Now print your trees onto the wrapping paper and decorate them with red and gold paint.

Pen-cap printing

Pen caps make pretty patterns.

Try using the eraser at the end of your pencil.

Use the base of your pen to make a big circle.

Camouflage kit

Print with a scrunched-up plastic bag to make it look like camouflage.

Marble paper

It's so good, the technique
needs to be kept a secret!

Marble effects

Marble paper looks so
impressive that it will
astound your friends,
AND it's really easy to do.
Once you have made it,
you can wrap things in
it, cover things with it,
use it as a frame,
write on it. You'll
impress everyone
you know with it!

The marble effect

Oil and water don't mix—that's how
the paint stays on the surface of the water—and
that's how it makes wiggly, marbly swirls on the
paper. If that doesn't make sense, don't worry;
just follow the instructions. You'll be amazed.

BAKING PAN
WITH WATER

OIL
PAINTS

PAPER
TOWELS

PAINT
CUPS

TURPENTINE

The paint mixture

Before you start, make the paint mixture.
Squeeze a blob of paint into a cup and add
four caps full of turpentine. Mix them
together. The paint will become very thin.

⭐ **Ask an adult**
to help mix the
paint with turpentine.

WHITE PAPER

TOOTHPICK

NEWSPAPER

3 Lay the paper on top
Let the paper just float on the water.

4 Push it down slightly
Gently push the paper to help it make contact.

1 Add the paint to some water

Pour about 1 in (2.5 cm) of water into the pan. Add a small teaspoon of each color of paint mixture.

2 Swirl the paint around

Dip a toothpick in and move it around in the mixture, but don't mix it!

5 Remove the paper

Pick up the corners and lift the paper out quickly.

6 Let it dry

Allow it to dry flat on a newspaper.

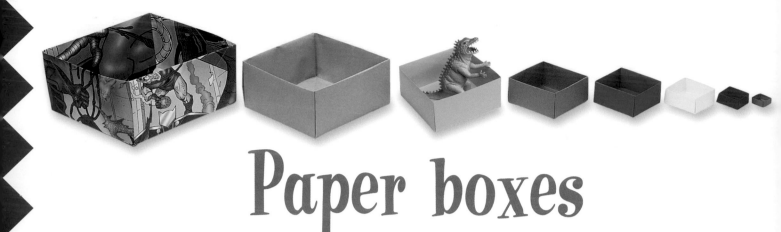

Paper boxes

What do you do if you need a box of a particular size? Simple: you make one yourself. You can choose the size and the color, too! Try using wrapping paper or homemade printed paper.

Making a block box

As you make each fold, be sure to press the fold down firmly so that when you open it, you can see the crease.

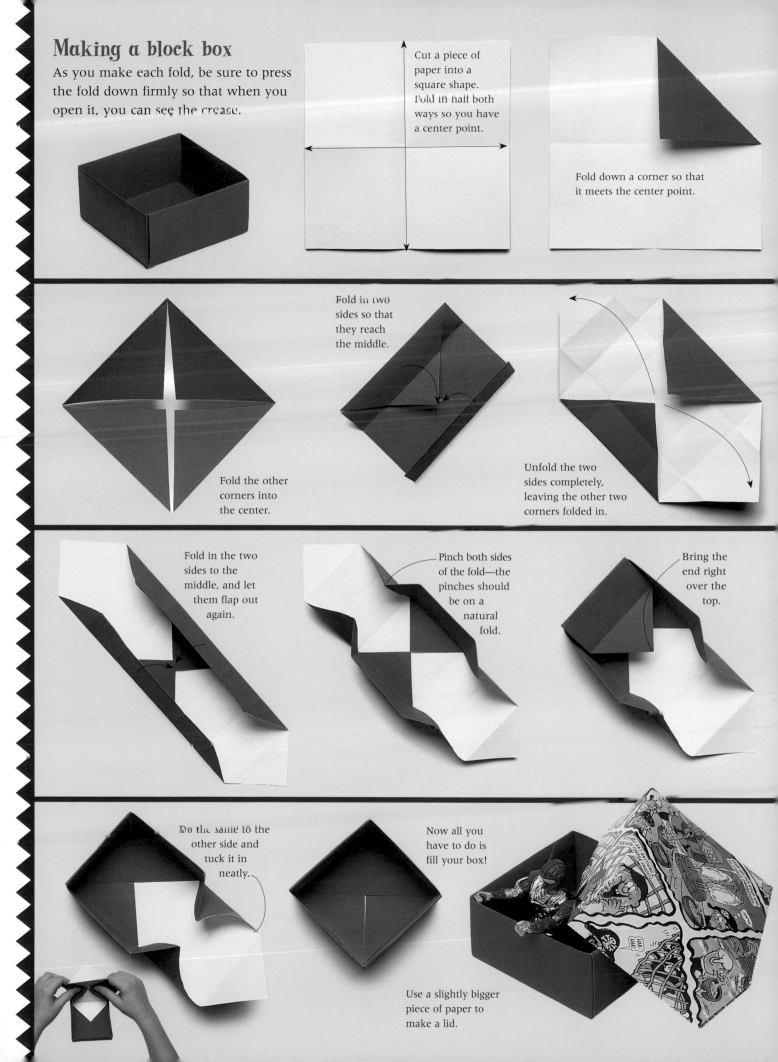

Cut a piece of paper into a square shape. Fold in half both ways so you have a center point.

Fold down a corner so that it meets the center point.

Fold the other corners into the center.

Fold in two sides so that they reach the middle.

Unfold the two sides completely, leaving the other two corners folded in.

Fold in the two sides to the middle, and let them flap out again.

Pinch both sides of the fold—the pinches should be on a natural fold.

Bring the end right over the top.

Do the same to the other side and tuck it in neatly.

Now all you have to do is fill your box!

Use a slightly bigger piece of paper to make a lid.

A star box

Stuff your star full of candies and other delicious treats.

To start...

fold a square piece of paper...

along these folds...

then unfold them again.

Hold the top and bottom corners and bring them together, making sure you tuck the two sides in.

The opening should be at the top.

It should be a diamond shape with two flaps in the middle.

Make sure the opening is at the top.

Fold one side along to the central fold.

Open up the small flap and press flat.

Make sure these two folds line up.

Tuck the left side of the small flap behind itself.

Now do the same to the other side.

Both sides should now look the same.

Turn it over so that the other side is showing.

Do the same with the flaps at the back.

The back should look exactly the same as the front.

Fold all four flaps down as far as they will go.

When you have folded two flaps down, pull the other two to the side and they will fold down, too.

Your box should start to open when you fold over the flaps.

With your hand underneath, push up the middle and it will miraculously turn into a box.

Neaten up the star flaps and FILL IT UP!

Try different sizes and colors. You could even try making them with your own printed paper.

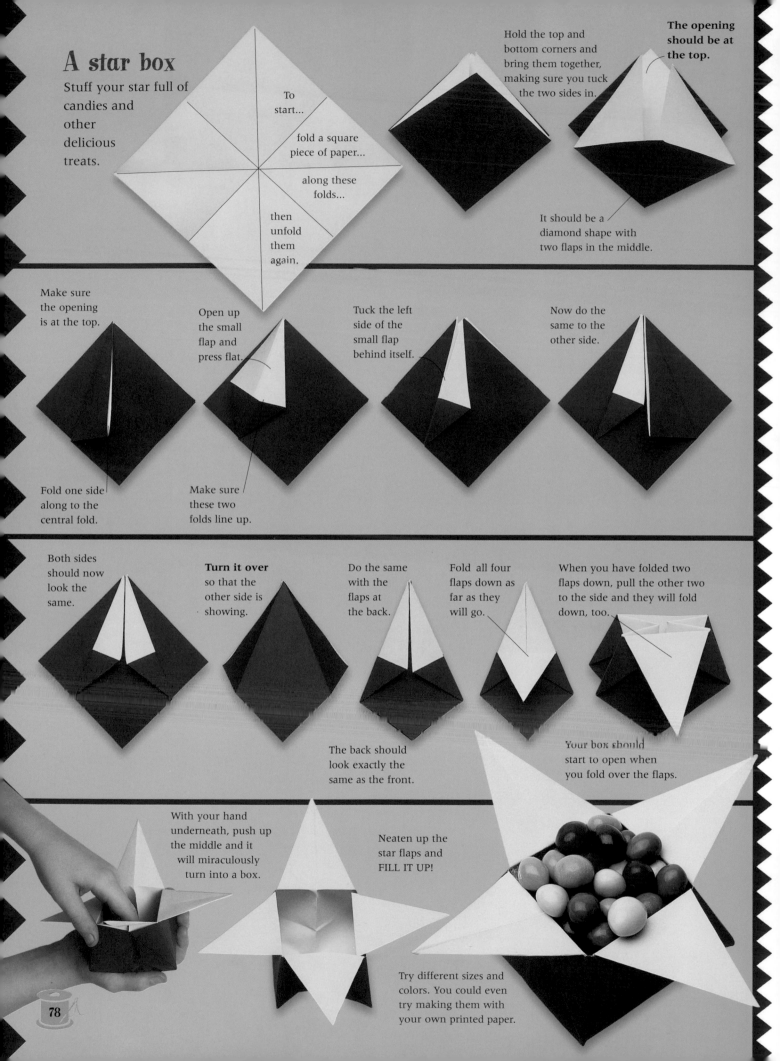

78

A galaxy of star boxes

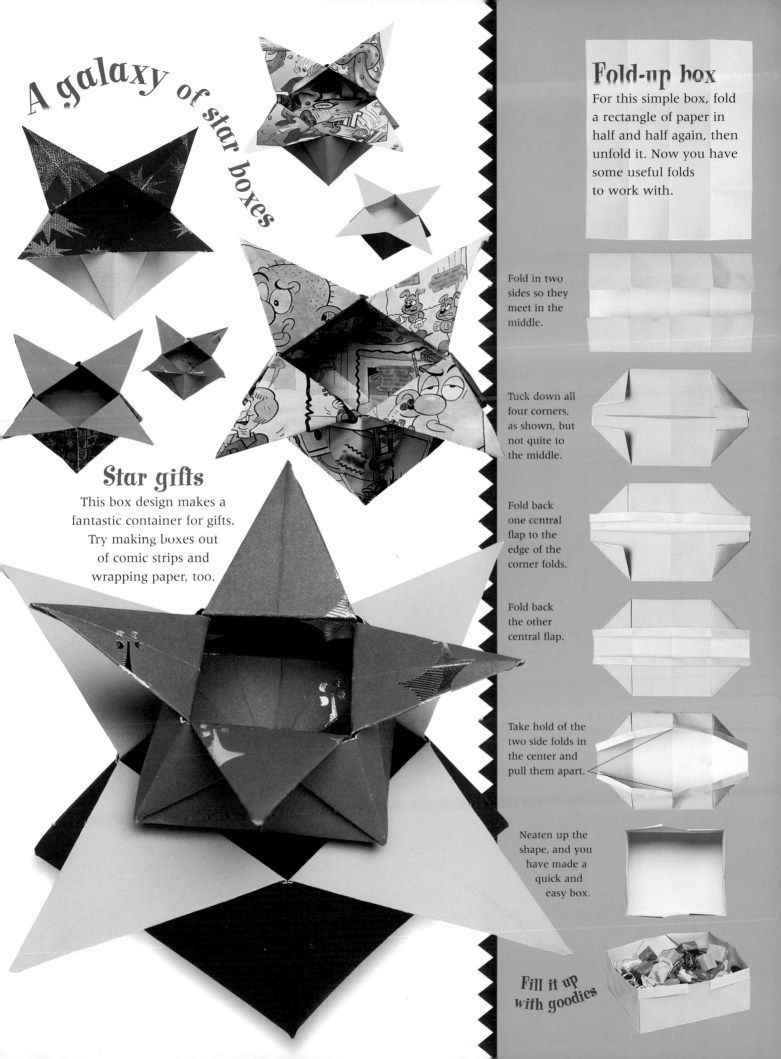

Star gifts

This box design makes a fantastic container for gifts. Try making boxes out of comic strips and wrapping paper, too.

Fold-up box

For this simple box, fold a rectangle of paper in half and half again, then unfold it. Now you have some useful folds to work with.

Fold in two sides so they meet in the middle.

Tuck down all four corners, as shown, but not quite to the middle.

Fold back one central flap to the edge of the corner folds.

Fold back the other central flap.

Take hold of the two side folds in the center and pull them apart.

Neaten up the shape, and you have made a quick and easy box.

Fill it up with goodies

Secret snowman

Surprise, surprise! What's hiding under his hat?

Secret snowballs

They're not just a pretty decoration to hang on the tree, but a secret stash of goodies! Give one to a friend and fill it with gifts.

Pull your snowball apart

...and let the goodies roll out

Off with his hat!

Look what's inside...

Make a paper pot

CRAFT GLUE

BALLOONS

TORN-UP NEWSPAPER

To stop the paper from sticking to the balloon, spread petroleum jelly on it.

1

Cover the balloon with craft glue.

2

Spread pieces of newspaper over the balloon, leaving the bottom uncovered.

3

Repeat steps 1 and 2 six more times. Finish with a layer of craft glue.

4

Leave it to dry for a day or two.

Use a jar to support it.

When it's hard and dry, pop the balloon.

Pop!

Make a secret snowman

You will need to start with two pots of the same size. Blow up your balloons to match. One will be for the hat and the other for the head.

2

HAT   HEAD

Trim them down

1

The dotted lines show where to trim them down.

First, make two pots

Paint and Glue

Mix equal amounts of paint with craft glue. This creates a nice sheen when it is dry and makes the pot stronger.

FOLD ALONG DOTTED LINES

Nose template

Trace the nose and cut it out of cardboard.

3

MASKING TAPE

Wrap it in masking tape.

Scrunch up some paper into a ball.

Use a strong glue to fix it in place.

Trim the hat

4

Stick on a folded paper nose with strong glue.

Paste some pieces of paper over the seams.

Add a nose

5

Paint them with white paint mixed with craft glue.

Leave them to dry

Paint them all white

6

Mix the paints with craft glue.

Give him a face

Make an ornament

Make two pots and this time blow up two smaller balloons the same size.

1 Make two small pots.

2 Trim them down.

Cover with white paint.

POT BASE   POT LID

3 Ask an adult to make a small hole in the bottom of each pot.

4 Decorate the pots with paint and glitter.

5 Take a piece of ribbon 22 in (60 cm) long and tie the two ends together.

Pass the ribbon up through the hole in the large pot.

Push the ribbon through the hole in the lid. Now you can hang your ornament.

A Winter Wonderland

Who would ever know

that these Christmassy characters in their wintery lands are more than just great-looking faces? Open them and see for yourself.

Hats off to penguins with presents!

Keep your head or you'll give away the secret!

Goodies Galore

Don't build just one snowman— make a whole family to guard the presents and keep extra treats safely inside. Create a forest of trees in a snowy land, filled to the brim with gifts and goodies.

The penguin and snowman chat happily, keeping their secrets under their hats!

How to Make Gift Boxes

Collect all kinds of tubes, big or small from potato chip canisters and cookie containers to toilet paper and paper towel rolls—all are perfect for your character boxes. The important thing is to fill them with candy and other little gifts and surprise someone on Christmas day.

Penguin Box

A large tube is perfect for making a performing penguin. When you have mastered the tricky parts, why not try making some smaller penguin chicks?

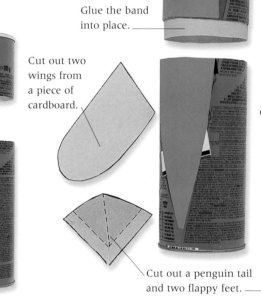

Cut off a third of the way down the tube.

Make a cardboard band and wrap it neatly inside the top part. This will keep the lid on.

Cut out two wings from a piece of cardboard.

Glue the band into place.

Measure a large beak to stick on the head.

Wing.

Cut out a penguin tail and two flappy feet.

Tape the features to the tube.

Festive Firs

Hang these trees up by their ribbons or sit them in a foresty lineup. Why not put them around the base of a Christmas tree?

Cut a semicircle of paper to make a cone big enough for your container.

Snip away to make a decorative edge.

Paint on some glue patterns and sprinkle them with glitter.

When it is dry, curl it into a cone and glue in place.

Fold a piece of ribbon in half and cut it so it is twice as long as the cone.

Thread on a bead and push it to the middle.

Penguin Suit

Put glue along the edge.

Make this edge long enough to fit around the top of the head with a 1/4 in (5 mm) overlap.

Try it on your penguin and trim it until it fits. Glue the sides together.

Glue the hat to the tube.

Add a band and pom-pom.

Give him some eyes.

Make clothes out of scraps of material.

Paint the penguin with acrylic paint and craft glue mixed together.

Paint the features using different colors.

Now fill your penguin!

Dressing the Snowman

Prepare a tube in the same way as the penguin box.

Tape on pipe cleaner arms.

Spread glue on the box and cover it with tufts of cotton balls.

Put a ribbon through the lid and tape it in place.

Try making a junior snowman with a small tube.

Decorate him with material scraps.

Cover a container with wrapping paper for the trunk of the tree.

Make a small hole in the top and thread the ribbon through it.

Pierce two holes in the container and tie the two ribbon ends through them.

Snap on the lid to keep the goodies locked up.

A forest of firs . . .

. . . filled with fancies

Christmas
scents

Sweet and spicy mixes of cinnamon and cloves with the fruity aroma of orange fill the air.

Pomanders and potpourri—perfect to give as presents.

Making scents

Rich, spicy smells are all around at Christmastime, so why not gather them up and bottle them?

Pour in the ingredients

Mix up a pot of scents

To make potpourri, spoon spices, such as nutmeg and pumpkin pie spice, into a jar. Add cinnamon sticks, pine cones, cloves, and other scents. Turn the jar over to mix everything. Store it in a cool, dry place and turn daily for several weeks.

Put on the lid.

Turn the jar each day.

Keep turning for weeks.

CINNAMON STICKS

ORRIS ROOT

PUMPKIN PIE SPICE

WHOLE NUTMEG

ALLSPICE BERRIES

STAR ANISE

Clove-studded oranges

These scented fruits are called pomanders. Oranges work best, but you could try other citrus fruits, too. The jeweled pomander will last only a few days, but the clove-studded orange will last for much longer.

You will need

PAPER BAG

RIBBON

CLOVES

LIME

LEMON

KUMQUATS

ORRIS ROOT

ORANGE

TANGERINE

MASKING TAPE

Wrap some tape around the middle of the orange.

Push the cloves in until the orange is covered.

GROUND
NUTMEG

GROUND CINNAMON

CINNAMON STICKS

PINE
CONES

WHOLE
CLOVES

After about six
weeks, your
potpourri will
be ready.

Some scent tips

POTPOURRI • Because the
ingredients are dry, it will last
forever, but the scent will fade after
a few months.

POMANDERS • As the orange dries
out, it will shrink and only the
cloves will show. It will smell nice
for weeks.

ORRIS ROOT • You can buy this in
health food stores. It's used to help
preserve the sweet smells.

Glass-
headed pins
and sequins.

Jeweled
pomander

Mix up the
pins and the
cloves for a
colorful,
jeweled
look.

Put the orris root
into a bowl.

Wrap the
orange in a
paper bag.

Remove the tape
and tie on a pretty
ribbon.

Roll the
orange
around until
it is coated.

Tape up the
top.

Leave in a warm,
dry place for six
weeks.

Packing Presents

It's the night before Christmas and, as dusk falls, stockings are waiting to be filled through the night. So surprise Santa with these bright ones!

Attach a loop at the top so that you can hang it.

Glue all of the decorations on with a fabric glue. The tube will say if the glue is suitable.

Cut out two sock shapes and glue them together with a fabric glue.

Make them big—Santa has lots of gifts this year!

Cut Rudolph's face shape out of felt and glue it to the stocking. Use different colors for the features.

A Stitch in Time

To jazz up the stocking, try your hand at blanket stitch around the edges.

Start the stitch by putting the needle through about 1/2 in (1 cm) away from the edge.

Bring the thread under the needle as you pull it down and through—it's as simple as that!

Fill me up to the brim

Stick 'em Up!

If the stockings are ready then it's almost Christmas day. Hurray! Hang them up for Santa to fill, or make one as a gift for someone special.

These felt snowflakes prove that you don't have to use a lot of colors to get a great Christmas look.

The best thing about these stockings is that you can use them year after year.

Eats and treats

Tuck into some reindeer cookies and rainbow cakes, create some Christmassy treats, and whisk up a meringue mountain for the ultimate festive feast.

Sugar and spice

Yum Yum

Spicy cookies
With a hint of orange, dipped in sweet icing.

97

Mix up some spice

Stir up the spice—these delicious cookies can be served right away or stored in an airtight container for a few weeks.

ASK AN ADULT to help with the oven.

Set the oven to 375°F (190°C).

Sugar

Butter

Mix them into a creamy mixture.

1 Cream together

Add all the ingredients.

Flour

Orange rind

Cinnamon

Ginger

2 Add the flavor

3 Mix it all up

Squeeze the mixture into a ball.

Wrap the ball in a plastic bag and put in the refrigerator for two hours.

4 Make a ball

Sprinkle some flour on the table.

Cut the ball in half.

Roll out the dough to ¼ in (5 mm) thick.

Cut out some shapes.

5 Roll it out

Make holes for ribbons with a straw.

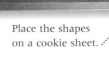

Place the shapes on a cookie sheet.

Put in the oven and bake for 15 minutes.

6 Shape and bake

¾ CUP (175 G) BUTTER

½ CUP BROWN SUGAR

1⅔ CUPS FLOUR

2 TEASPOONS GINGER

2 TEASPOONS CINNAMON

GRATED ORANGE RIND

7 Now decorate

Remove them from the oven and put them on a rack to cool.

Sugar and water icing

When the cookies are cold, decorate them with icing. Mix 3 tablespoons of confectioners' sugar and 3 teaspoons of water. Decorate with silver balls, or any tasty decorations that you like.

Spoon on the icing and smooth it out.

Make a snowman cookie

Cookie cutters

Cut two circles.   Join together.   Decorate.

Santa's on the Move

Jingle bells! Santa's on his way. Give him a little time to fill his sleigh with goodies and he'll be up in the sky in a flash.

☆ Candy Factory

All it takes to create Santa's chalet and sleigh are lots of goodies and a little imagination. When you have built your sleigh, fill it with bundles of bright candies and cookies—don't be tempted to eat them—and display them on the Christmas table.

Sugar snow sprinkled through a paper doily provides a snowy landscape for the reindeer to visit

HOW TO BUILD SANTA'S CHALET AND SLEIGH

All you need is a piece of cardboard for the sleigh base and a milk carton for the chalet.

Cookie layer glued down.

Cardboard base.

Bars of chocolate.

Chocolate mini-rolls and fingers.

Sugary Glue

Mix confectioners' sugar and water to make a sticky paste. Spread it on with a knife and press your cookies down on top of it.

Cut off the bottom of the carton if it is too tall.

Paste on chocolate fingers as logs for the house.

A cracker makes a good front to start building on.

Sticky Tip

If your roof keeps slipping down, put the box in the refrigerator for a few minutes until the icing hardens.

Candy canes for speedy runners

Remember to leave enough room on the base for the runners.

A cookie back rest for Santa.

Use jelly beans and gumdrops for decoration.

Santa's Cookie Factory

Ho, ho, ho, Santa's been busy rustling up some tasty truffles to tickle the tastebuds.

⭐ Rudolph's Truffles

1/2 cup (125 g) melted butter
3 cups crushed
graham crackers
4 tablespoons coconut
4 tablespoons cocoa
4 tablespoons honey

Mix all the ingredients together in the pan

Yum Yum

Ask an adult . .
⭐ *to melt the butter*

Crush the cookies in a bag

⭐ Easy as 1-2-3

The best thing about the truffles is that once the butter has melted there's no more cooking. Ask an adult to melt the butter while you crush the crackers. Let the pan cool before you add the rest of the ingredients.

Wash your hands . .
⭐ *before you touch the mixture*

Pour onto a cookie sheet

Divide the mixture into squares with a knife.

Put the sheet in the refrigerator for a few hours.

Roll the squares into balls

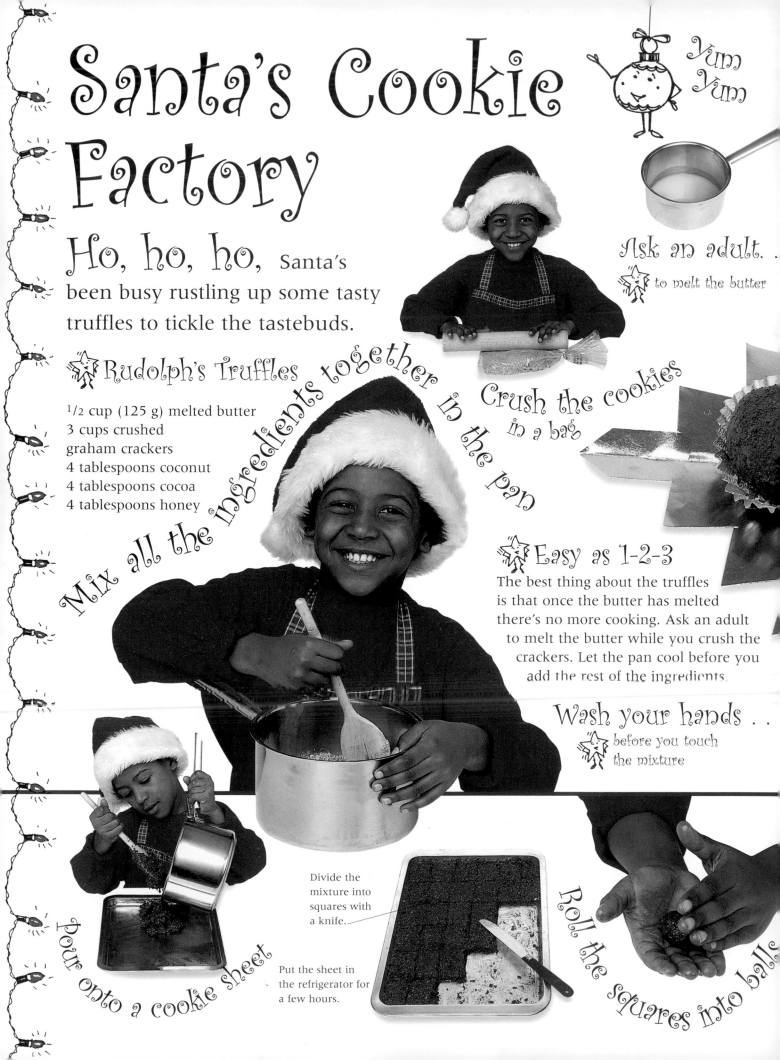

Magic Marzipan

To make truffle Santas, mix a few drops of food coloring into some marzipan and shape into Santa's features. Try marzipan holly leaves and berries as well for extra plate decoration.

squeeze, roll, and shape into Santa's features

Cover your truffles with delicious decorations

Coconut, chopped nuts, cocoa, or grated chocolate— anything you can think of!

Roll the truffles and place them in paper baking cups.

103

Rainbow cupcakes

Heaps of colorful rainbow cupcakes cover the party table. Bake cupcakes and decorate them as magically as you can.

Conjure up Colorful Cupcakes

A measure, a whisk, and the swish of a wand.

¹/₂ cup
self-rising flour

¹/₂ cup (125 g)
butter (room
temperature)

¹/₂ cup
superfine sugar

1 teaspoon baking powder

2 eggs

1 teaspoon vanilla extract

😊 Makes 24 cupcakes

CUPCAKE UTENSILS

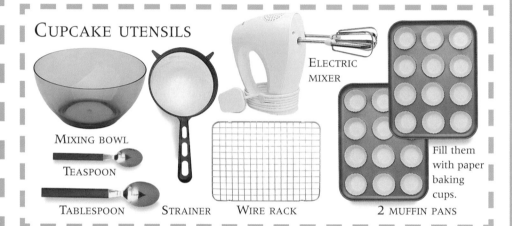

MIXING BOWL

TEASPOON

TABLESPOON

STRAINER

WIRE RACK

ELECTRIC MIXER

Fill them with paper baking cups.

2 MUFFIN PANS

Rainbow icing

😊 To ice 4 cupcakes

Mix up lots of little bowls of different colored icing.
For green icing, mix yellow and blue; for orange,
mix yellow and red. Use sweets to decorate the tops,
such as candied cherries, raisins, or sprinkles.

1 tablespoon
confectioners' sugar
1 teaspoon water
1 drop food coloring

1. Mix the water, food
coloring, and
confectioners'
sugar.

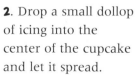

2. Drop a small dollop
of icing into the
center of the cupcake
and let it spread.

3. Decorate the cupcakes
with anything sweet
and use tubes of writing
icing for extra patterns.

Sifting adds more air

1. Sift the flour and baking powder

⭐ Set the oven to 375°F/190°C.

5. Fill the cups

Put a teaspoon of mixture in each.

⏰ Bake in the oven for 20 minutes.

3. Beat until creamy

2. Add everything else

Beat the eggs and throw them in with the butter, sugar, and vanilla extract.

4. Does it drop off a spoon?

If it drops off easily in a dollop, then it's ready.

6. Take out of the oven

⭐ Ask an adult to help with this step.

Shhh... cupcakes cooling

meringue mountain

whisk up egg whites into sweet frothy peaks to make delicious desserts.

Egg whites
2 whites

+

Superfine sugar
⅔ cup

=

Makes about
12 small peaks

108

Fruity nest

Spoon whipped cream onto a nest and top it off with pieces of fruit.

peak sandwich

Sandwich two meringue peaks together with whipped cream.

Mmmmeringue

Meringues are made from egg whites mixed with sugar and baked in a cool oven until they are crunchy on the outside and soft inside—mmmm!

Serve your meringues with cream and fruit, or just plain and simple.

It's ready when you can turn the bowl upside down without the egg whites sliding off.

Use a big clean bowl.

Use the mixer at top speed.

3 Is it ready?

1 Beat the egg whites

2 Keep mixing

whisk up a mountain

An electric mixer makes the egg whites froth up quicker than whisking by hand. Make sure the beaters have stopped spinning before you take them out of the bowl, or you'll make a mess!

Meringue hints and tips

• Whisk the egg whites just enough—try the "upside-down" test in step 3.
• Add the sugar a tablespoon at a time while beating the egg whites. Keep repeating this until all the sugar is used up.
• Grease the sheet first to stop the paper from slipping.

Grease the tray, then cover with parchment paper.

Preheat the oven to 275°F (140°C).

7 Spoon out some meringue

Pour in the sugar—about a tablespoon at a time.

4 Add sugar and mix

Beat in the sugar BUT not at full speed.

5 Keep mixing

When all the sugar is in, mix it one last time.

The mixture should look glossy and stand up in peaks.

6 It's peaked!

EQUIPMENT

MIXING BOWL

ELECTRIC MIXER

TEASPOON AND TABLESPOON

PARCHMENT PAPER

BAKING SHEET

PASTRY BRUSH

Press the peak down with a spoon to make a nest.

Make a snowman with peaks joined together.

 Bake in the oven for 2 hours.

8 Ready to bake

Take the meringues out of the oven.

Leave them for a few hours to dry.

9 All dried out

Sweets and treats

Dig in to minty snowballs and Rudolph chocolates all laid out on a plate, or wrap them up sweetly to give away as tasty gifts. . . yum yum!

Chocolate Rudolphs

You will need:

ALMOND HALVES

CANDIED CHERRY HALVES

JELLY CANDY STRIPS

SILVER BALLS

CHOCOLATE 6 OZ (170 G)

COOKIE SHEET AND WAX PAPER

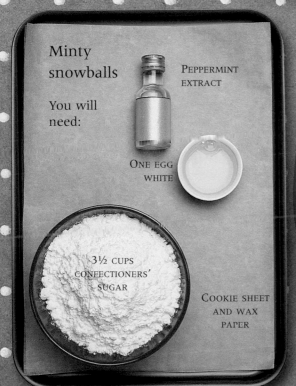

Minty snowballs

You will need:

PEPPERMINT EXTRACT

ONE EGG WHITE

3½ CUPS CONFECTIONERS' SUGAR

COOKIE SHEET AND WAX PAPER

Making sweet treats

Chocolate Rudolphs

Melt the chocolate over a bowl of hot water.

Fill the bowl with boiling water.

Ask an adult to help with the hot water.

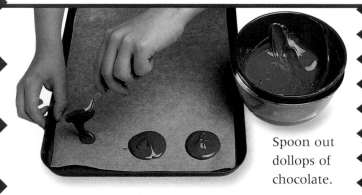

Spoon out dollops of chocolate.

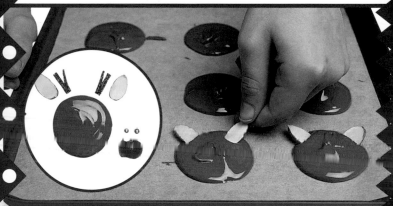

Before the chocolate sets, add Rudolph's face.

Leave them to set.

Minty snowballs

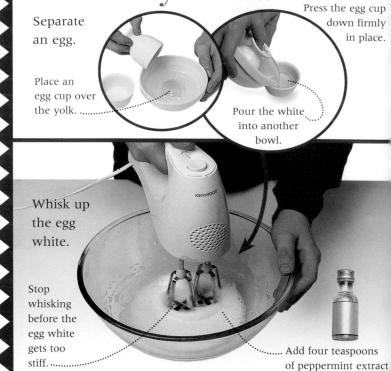

Separate an egg.

Place an egg cup over the yolk.

Press the egg cup down firmly in place.

Pour the white into another bowl.

Whisk up the egg white.

Stop whisking before the egg white gets too stiff.

Add four teaspoons of peppermint extract

Add the egg white to the sugar

Mix it all together.

Make into a ball.

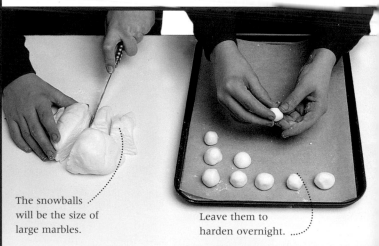

The snowballs will be the size of large marbles.

Cut up the ball.

Leave them to harden overnight.

Make some snowballs.

Make some gifts

Use the projects in this book to create presents for your family and friends.

...Up, up, and away

Chilly treats

These secret pots can hold whatever you want. Keep the snowman and bring him out year after year.

Put your cookies in an air-tight container and they will last a few weeks longer.

Gifts to eat

Decorate a cookie tin and fill it with your spicy stars • A felt stocking can be filled with goodies and hung on the tree • Wrap up some minty snowballs in a cellophane bundle • Fill the snowmen with anything you want to give away

Leave the top of the sock open

Festive fortune

Potpourri will keep its scent if sealed in a jar until it's time to give it away.

Fill felt ornaments with dried lavender and sew them up.

You can fill a plastic bag with your mints.

Mint bundle

Gather it up at the top and tie with a ribbon.

Scented gifts

Decorate a jar of pot-pourri with a bright, festive ribbon • Present pomanders in pretty boxes plumped up with tissue paper or fabric and finished off with a ribbon • Stuff your felt shapes with dried lavender for a scented decoration

Remember, the more cloves you use, the longer your pomanders will last.

Pretty pomander sits in a special box.

Index

Acknowledgments

Dorling Kindersley would like to thank Maisie Armah, Charlotte Bull,
Billy Bull, James Bull, Daniel Ceccarelli, Lulu Coulter, Seriya Ezigwe,
Harry Holmstoel, Sorcha Lyons, and Kailen Wilcox for being merry models
and Penny Arlon for text and editing.

Additional photography: Dave King for the magician on page 56,
the fairy and the pantomime horse on page 57. Steve Shott for the carol
singers on pages 51 and 56.

All other images © Dorling Kindersley.
For further information see:
www.dkimages.com

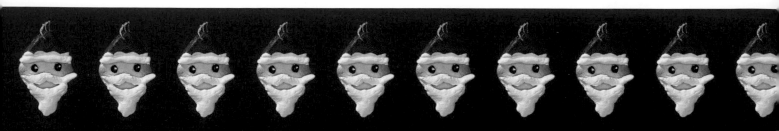